Merry Christmas 1985
To Brian & Janice Beals
from Dad & Mother Beals

WHAT WILL TOMORROW BRING?

the *Life-Story* of

RALPH AND ESTHER CHOATE

by

Betty M. Hockett

GEORGE FOX PRESS
P.O. BOX 44 • NEWBERG, OREGON 97132

TO GENE,

who helps make it possible for his wife
to write books and other things.

WHAT WILL TOMORROW BRING?

The LIFE-STORY of Ralph and Esther Choate

© 1985 George Fox Press
Library of Congress Catalog Card Number: 85-70504
ISBN: 0-913342-49-1

Cover by Lois A. Nelson
Illustrations by Phyllis M. Cammack

Litho in U.S.A. by The Barclay Press, Newberg, Oregon

CONTENTS

Ralph and Esther Choate

Chapter 1

ALMOST TOO LATE

On an August Sunday afternoon in 1925, Ralph Edgar Choate, age seventeen, lay motionless on his bed in Greenleaf, Idaho.

For many days a high fever had raged through his body. And now he was almost completely paralyzed.

Ralph's mother sat down gently on the side of her son's bed. "Ralph," she said quietly. "The doctor has determined you have the dreadful disease called polio. That's why you can't move. And Ralph . . ." Mrs. Choate could hardly go on. She wiped her tears away with the corner of her apron. "The doctor says the paralysis may be spreading to your brain. That means . . . ." Her voice cracked again. "You . . . you could die at any time."

"I'm not afraid to die," Ralph thought as he lay there suffering.

At that same time, Pastor Calvin Choate, Ralph's father, stood before the Sunday evening congregation at the Greenleaf Friends Church. "As

1

you know, Ralph is very ill," he said. "I don't feel that I can preach tonight. I need to be home with my family."

The congregation understood. One man immediately got up and suggested, "We'll spend the time here in prayer for Ralph."

The people got down on their knees. "Dear God, if it is Your will, please make Ralph well," they prayed.

That evening, Calvin and Louie Choate and their younger daughter Dorothy sat quietly near Ralph's bedside. The hours dragged by!

Suddenly they could not believe their ears. "Mother! I want a drink!" It was Ralph's voice. He had not been able to speak that clearly for the last two days.

Mrs. Choate rushed to get the water for Ralph. She watched him swallow for the first time since he had become paralyzed on Friday.

"Praise the Lord!" Calvin Choate's big voice boomed out heartily.

The next morning, Ralph could swallow almost normally. Soon everyone in Greenleaf knew God had answered prayer. "His recovery is really a miracle!" the people reminded each other.

When the doctor examined Ralph again, he too said, "It's a miracle you are alive. You know, bulbar poliomyelitis is a *very* serious illness."

Ralph spent the next year getting well. Although his left arm had not been affected, he had to work hard to make his right arm useful again. With a lot of effort he relearned how to write. Little by little, his legs began to move, but his right ankle remained paralyzed.

He had to figure out a new way to put one foot in front of the other in order to walk. It was not easy. Some days Ralph felt discouraged. But he faithfully exercised day after day.

"See, I can do it!" he said courageously. "I lift my right leg, then swing the foot out." Step . . . step . . . step! Slowly, holding tightly to a walker his father had constructed for him—but he *was* walking.

His family helped him in every way possible. Mrs. Choate kept Ralph's older sister Mildred, who was away at college, informed of his progress. "He's standing with the help of crutches now," said one letter. Then later she wrote, "Ralph walked over to church today for the first time since he was sick. He walked down the aisle, too. People were so happy to see him!"

Ralph remained cheerful through the long recovery. He did not complain—even when he watched a football game, the sport he had especially loved to play.

While he was getting well, Ralph had lots of time to think about God and what He wanted him to do. He had accepted Jesus as his Savior when he was a very small boy in Indiana. For a long time he had planned to be a missionary in Africa.

Life was different now. He had to use two canes in order to walk. "But these canes won't stop me from obeying God," he said with determination. "I still intend to serve Him in Africa."

*   *   *

It was also during the summer of 1925 that another important event took place—far away in Kenya, Africa.

Eighteen-year-old Esther Chilson was attending a special conference held for the Africans at Kaimosi (Ky-moe-see). Esther was there because she was the daughter of Arthur and Edna Chilson, missionaries in Kenya. Esther had already asked Jesus to be her Savior as she and her sister Rachel were growing up in Kenya. While she was at this conference, Esther heard God talking to her.

"Esther," He said. "I want your life *completely*."

"Yes, God," she replied. "I will be completely Yours. I love You with all my heart and I'll do exactly what You want me to do."

Then God asked, "Are you willing to be a missionary to India?"

Esther was startled! "India? But God, I've always planned to be a missionary here in Kenya. I already know the language. I know the people. I don't want to go to India!"

Right off she did not like this new idea at all. A real struggle went on in her heart. It was hard to give up her dream of staying in the land she knew and loved. She thought about it a lot.

Before the conference was over, though, Esther answered, "Yes, Lord. If that's what you want, I will

4

go to India. I can learn to work with the people there. I can learn to love them."

"Thank you, Esther," God said. "I wanted to see if you were really willing to do whatever I asked. Now I know." Then she was glad to hear God say, "Esther, I want you to serve Me in Africa."

*   *   *

Several summers later, Ralph Choate and Esther Chilson met once again at Twin Rocks, Oregon. (They had first met when they were four years old, and because their families were friends, they had seen each other now and then.) As they attended the Friends Conference at the beach, the two college-age young people had opportunity to become better acquainted.

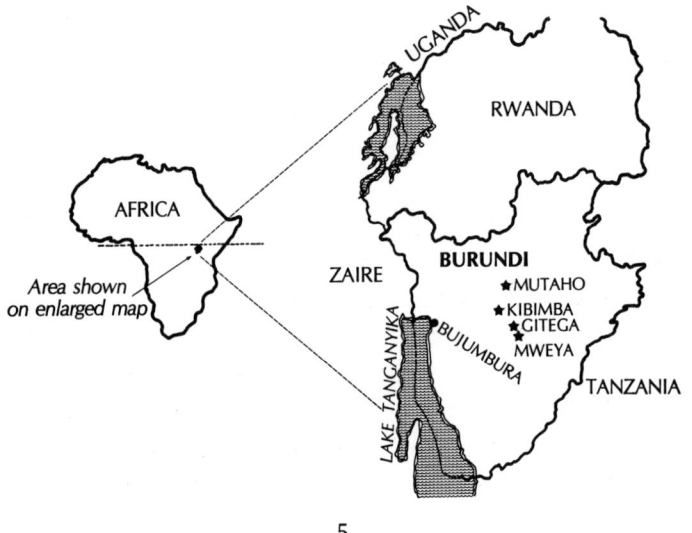

"For as long as I can remember I've planned to go to Africa," Ralph explained to Esther. "When I was five years old I told my parents, 'I'm going to go way down yonder and preach a great big preach.'"

Esther told Ralph about her plans. "God has called me to be a missionary in Africa, too."

Their interest in each other developed rapidly before Esther went back home to Kansas. There she finished college at Friends University. Ralph graduated from Pacific College (now George Fox College) in Newberg, Oregon.

Soon the two realized they were in love. On August 15, 1932, they were married. "We plan to go to Africa as soon as possible," they happily announced to family and friends.

Until it was time to go to Africa, they lived in Greenleaf, Idaho. Ralph taught at the Friends Academy, from which he had graduated several years before.

One day while she was on the way to the store, Esther discovered a nickel on the hard-packed dirt road.

"This can be the beginning of our Africa fund," Ralph suggested when she showed it to him.

Esther hurried to get a little clay cup she had brought from Africa. "We'll put the nickel in here. Any extra money we have can go in, too."

Ralph and Esther were occasionally invited to churches to tell about the new Friends mission in Burundi, a very small country in Africa. Sometimes

after a service, people handed them a dollar. Each time the money promptly went into the clay cup.

Before long, Kansas Yearly Meeting of Friends said, "We want you to be our missionaries in Burundi."

Ralph and Esther gladly replied, "Yes! This is what God wants us to do!"

By then their Africa fund had grown until they could pay for dental work, new eyeglasses, physical examinations, and shots that were necessary to protect them from malaria and other diseases. After all that, there was enough money left to pay for their tickets on the big ship.

At last it was time to go!

Early in the morning of November 13, 1935, they found themselves in a frenzy of activity in New York City.

Soon after breakfast they walked twenty-five blocks to the *uptown* office of the company that owned the ship they would soon board.

"I'm sorry," said the woman at the desk. "Your passport and papers are at the *downtown* office."

Ralph and Esther hurried down there as fast as they could. When they arrived, they discovered that only part of their papers were there.

"The other forms have been mislaid in an office far away in Chicago," the secretary reported. Some papers had not been filled out at all. Telegrams were quickly sent and the answers came back promptly. It looked as if everything could be finished up in time to board the ship as scheduled.

Then came another delay. One official who had to sign his name to their papers was not there yet. Ralph and Esther looked uneasily at the clock.

Just when they had nearly given up hope, the man arrived. He signed his name and everything was finally completed at 10:35.

"Thank you for helping us," Ralph and Esther said, quickly handing over the money they owed. Immediately they dashed out to the street, hired a taxi and rode off to get their baggage.

At 11:20 they breathlessly walked up the gangplank. Forty minutes later, at exactly twelve o'clock noon, the big ship chugged away from Pier 60.

"We were almost too late!" said Ralph.

He and Esther stood on deck, watching New York City melt into the fog. They smiled at each other, grateful that they were going to Africa together.

Soon all familiar sights had vanished. They turned their faces toward the bow of the ship. At that moment they had no idea what the next tomorrows would bring, far far ahead in their new home—Burundi, Africa.

Chapter 2

THE WALLS CAME TUMBLING DOWN

"This is the hand-shakingest bunch of people I've ever seen in all my life," Ralph whispered to Esther.

"It's the European custom," she explained. "Remember, Burundi is under the rule of Belgium. A Belgian must shake hands with you when he comes and when he goes."

More Africans than they could count had just walked by. Each one shook hands and greeted the new missionaries. "Good day! How are you?"

Ralph and Esther's first glimpse of the Kibimba (Key-BEAM-ba) mission station and the people who lived round about came on December 31, 1935. It stood high on a hill, overlooking many valleys. All around were more hills.

Esther's parents, Arthur and Edna Chilson, and her sister, Rachel, had lived there since April 1934. At that time the Belgian government had said, "You have permission to organize the Friends Africa Gospel Mission." Without that permission, it would

9

have been illegal for the mission to own property. They could not have invited missionaries to come.

By the time the Choates arrived, the Chilsons had completed their own brick house. They also had constructed a small two-room brick house for Ralph and Esther. The 5,000 eucalyptus (uke-a-LIP-tus) trees, 550 coffee trees, and many peach trees were growing well. Guava, orange, and lime trees were looking good, also. Bright, exotic tropical flowers made splashes of color here and there on the green lawns.

"Burundi is one of the most beautiful countries in Africa. It's very small, with many gorges, water-falls, mountains, and valleys," the Choates wrote home to friends. "There is just one large city, Bujumbura, the capital. Even though the land is very steep, people farm small pieces of ground. The women are the farmers."

The letter went on to describe how the African families lived on their own plots of ground rather than in villages. Their houses were little igloo-shaped huts covered with grass, each surrounded by a closed-in area called an *urugo* (oo-ROO-go). Families carefully kept their possessions inside the *urugo*. Banana trees growing close around usually hid the hut completely.

Their letter also explained, "We arrived during the rainy season, September until mid-May. The dry season will begin before long. We're told it will be windy and cold then. We wish you could see some of the beautiful trees and bushes here. They have strange names such as bougainvillea, hibiscus, frangipani, bark cloth, and flamboyant. Many kinds of palm trees grow here, too. There's one called the 'traveler's tree.' It always has water at the base of the leaf stalk."

Ralph and Esther soon became acquainted with many uninvited visitors. Lizards, flies, mosquitos,

worms, and cockroaches came right in, along with termites that ate everything in sight. Snakes were an ever-present threat.

It was easy for the Choates to love the friendly, chocolate-brown or black, kinky-haired Africans who were called Barundi. It did not take long for the newcomers to learn that there were actually three groups of Barundi.

The Batutsi (Bah-TOOT-see) were the high class, the rulers. The Bahutu (Bah-HOO-too), or middle class, made the roads, farmed, and did some government work. The group called the Batwa (BOUGHT-wa) were the lowest class. They made clay pots and woven mats, which they traded for food.

They all spoke the Kirundi (Key-ROON-dee) language.

"This is certainly a difficult language," remarked Ralph to Esther. "I suppose it's easy for you, though, since you already know the language from Kenya."

Esther shook her head. "Not easy, Ralph. It's quite a separate language from what I learned there."

They studied the language as they worked at other daily duties. Ralph hung his notebook of Kirundi words on a nail in the workshop. As he sawed boards and built furniture he practiced the new words.

One day he needed to say something in Kirundi to the workmen. He thought carefully about what words to use.

"Put this manure on my heart," he said. Right away the men recognized his funny mistake and laughed loudly.

"You said *mutima* (heart), they corrected. "You should have said *mulima* (garden)."

Then Ralph remembered. Many of the Kirundi words sound almost like other Kirundi words, but they have entirely different meanings.

Ralph soon learned the language well enough to teach, preach, and do business. Since Esther already had an African accent, she became excellent with Kirundi. Even the Africans could be fooled as to who was talking if they did not see her. As the years went on, she maintained a good vocabulary. She taught Kirundi to many people. Eventually she was chosen to help give the Kirundi examinations to them, also. Because she was good at preaching in the language, she became a popular speaker at Sunday services and special meetings.

One day's mail brought a letter from a small church in western Kansas, alerting the Chilsons and the Choates that they would soon receive an unusual gift. "We are no longer needing the big bell that has rung out faithfully for many years here at the Prairie Flower Friends Church, so we are shipping the bell to you at Kibimba."

Arthur Chilson and Ralph Choate went into action right away. "We'll need to build a proper tower for the bell," they decided.

"Black wattle trees will be just right for poles to put the platform on," said Mr. Chilson. "That wood is hard and it won't rot soon. It'll last a long time because termites won't eat it, either."

The missionary men and their African helpers cut the tall poles, set them firmly in the ground, then constructed a platform.

The bell, four feet across at the bottom and weighing about 600 pounds, survived its long journey. Then came the hardest job of all—getting the heavy bell up onto the high tower.

The men designed "tracks," made from more poles, and carefully slid the bell into position. At last it was safely in place and securely bolted down.

"Listen to that wonderful sound!" said Ralph as the clear air dispersed the bell tones far out across the hills and valleys. For many years the bell from Kansas called the Barundi to worship.

Many Africans were glad that the missionaries had come to Kibimba. They came to the classes, and showed up to receive medicine that would make them well. However, not everyone appreciated the missionaries. The witch doctors were not pleased with them. The Catholic priests were not happy, either. They felt threatened by the presence of these outsiders whose teachings they did not understand.

A few weeks after their arrival, Ralph and Esther heard a frightening announcement one morning.

"They're coming to kill you!" shouted a woman frantically. "In a few days they'll beat their drums and then kill you!"

The woman sobbed hysterically. "The Catholic priests around here promised they'll round up all the local members of their church and come to beat you to death!" She put her hands over her face in despair.

The missionaries looked at each other. "We'll go on about our duties as usual," they said firmly. "God will take care of us."

"A threat like that *does* make a peculiar feeling come to one's stomach," Esther admitted.

"Sure does!" Ralph agreed.

The next days passed quietly with fewer people than usual coming to the mission. Catholics at their schools beat the drums loud and long one evening, but no crowd assembled for the promised beatings.

"Thank You, God, for keeping us safe," the missionaries prayed.

The Friends Africa Gospel Mission was the second Protestant group to become residents in Burundi. (The Danish Baptist Missionary Society arrived a few years before.) During those first years, the people who became Protestants were either directly from the pagan religions or from the Roman Catholic church.

"I want to be a Christian," said one Catholic man who came to the mission. He took off two aluminum bangles that were symbols of his church. "Here are my rosary beads and my Catholic registration card, too." The man also handed over his schoolbook.

"You have shown us you really mean what you say," the missionaries replied. "We'll hang these things up for all to see." Then they signed him on as a student at the Friends Men's School.

After that, many Africans became Protestants. They learned to love God and accept Christ as their Savior.

"The things you teach us about God are very different from what we learned in our old church," the converted Catholics told the missionaries. "The priests don't like what you are doing. They want to get rid of you Protestants."

The Catholics did all they could to frighten the new Christians and to make life difficult for them. It was a long time before they realized they could not defeat Protestantism. Gradually, through the years, the Catholics learned to accept the Protestants.

They even became friendly with them. They no longer felt threatened.

Before long, there were over 1,000 people coming to Sunday morning services at Kibimba. On Sunday afternoons the missionaries directed another service. People who came then wanted to learn more about the Christian faith. In that service, the missionaries told the people how to ask God to forgive them. They helped the Africans understand how to obey God. The chapel was usually full of interested people.

Just before time to begin the "seeker's service" one Sunday, the wind suddenly blew furiously. Heavy rain poured down with it.

"What's going on?" Ralph asked, looking out from their house. He was dismayed at what he saw.

"Esther, come quick! The wind blew the chapel down. The walls are all in a big heap!"

The Choates and the Chilsons ran outside to see if anything could be rescued. Africans who had been on their way hurried to help, too. Some carried the new organ to a storage shed. Others rushed about gathering reading books and other items into safety.

By that time, everyone was soaked by the rain.

"Thank God the storm didn't hit a few minutes later," said Ralph. "We would all have been inside the chapel. When the walls came tumbling down, no one could have gotten out safely."

*   *   *

Ralph and Esther became busier all the time. They had many new experiences, never knowing what tomorrow would bring. They learned how to do things they had never done before, such as pulling teeth. (At the end of ten years, Ralph's record book showed that he had pulled at least 1,000 teeth every year. Esther had pulled almost that many.)

There were sad times. They went with Chilsons to a nearby village for the burial of a two-year-old girl. It was the first Christian burial the Barundi had witnessed.

There were happy times, as well. "One of our young men is planning to get married," wrote Ralph in a letter. "It's quite interesting to us because he hasn't seen the girl yet. This seems to be the custom, although he thinks he might go have a look at her before the wedding day." According to the usual practice, the groom had to pay a sum of money for his bride. It was reported that this young man agreed to pay an amount equal to about $2.16 in American money.

Many events brought great blessings. The organization of the African church at Kibimba was a special time. Most of those taken into membership were very new Christians.

Ralph and Esther always had love in their hearts for all who said, "I want to be a Christian." There was love, also, for those who continued to worship trees, snakes, rocks, and animals. "Please help them want to be Christians, too," the Choates prayed.

It seemed such a short while until they had been in Burundi for a whole year. That first year had included many interesting adventures, but even more were yet to come!

Chapter 3

MUSIC
BRINGS A CROWD

Larry Chilson Choate was born to Ralph and Esther on the first day of March 1937. He was dedicated to the Lord at the Kibimba church a few days later. Grandfather Arthur Chilson performed the special dedication service. Grandmother Edna Chilson, who was also a minister, assisted. The arrival of their first child brought great joy to Ralph and Esther.

The African Christians made them feel happy, also. Many of them were learning to read, write, and sew. They were memorizing gospel songs and Bible verses.

Within a year there were 900 women and girls coming to the sewing classes. Each time they came, they heard more about God.

The mission continued to grow in every way. New buildings were constructed. Many Africans accepted Jesus as their Savior. Other missionaries arrived to join the Chilsons and the Choates.

They began making plans for more mission stations.

"The property on the mountain called Mutaho (Moo-TAH-hoe) seems like a good location," they decided. "There are thousands of people who won't hear the Gospel unless we go up there."

"May we be the ones to begin the work at Mutaho?" Ralph and Esther asked.

"Yes!" the others replied.

Ralph and Esther were pleased. "We know God has been and is with us here at Kibimba. He will be with us at Mutaho, too. He will not fail us nor forsake us."

Soon Ralph traveled the twenty-one difficult miles on an old and mostly unused road from Kibimba to the new hilltop site. He started a small building that would be their first home there. Each time he went, he stayed several days. Esther and little Larry remained at home.

Along with all there was to do at both places, Ralph and Esther were soon to experience sorrow and joy, one right after the other.

Early in 1939, Arthur Chilson died after being sick for only a few days. Ralph helped prepare the grave, and the faithful missionary was buried near the Kibimba church the next evening. More than 4,000 people came to mourn for their beloved friend.

"We needed him so much in the work here," said Ralph sadly. However, he and Esther knew the Friends mission work her father had helped to start in Burundi would continue with God's help.

A month later, on February 24, Ralph, Esther, and Larry welcomed Ann Lee into their family. Right from the beginning, the new baby added brightness to their home.

As he continued his journeys to Mutaho, Ralph hired workers to assist him. One morning, two African men appeared. "We're Catholics," they informed him. "We are not happy about working for a strange Protestant."

"I will pay you fairly," Ralph explained. "You'll receive the regular wage plus a gift of trading salt once a week."

Salt was precious. The idea of it being added to their wages pleased the men. Ralph also promised, "I will teach you how to make bricks and how to build homes and shops." Finally the two agreed.

Ralph wrote their names in his book. Simon Sodiya (So-DEE-ya) was the big, strong-looking man. The smaller worker was named Peter Rurajenguye (ROO-ra-jeng-GOO-yay). For a long time these men were just ordinary workmen. However, they learned well, developing into skilled workers. Before long they became Christians.

Ralph and Esther had classes after work hours so the men could learn to read and write. Eventually these two became pastors in the Friends Africa Gospel Church. They were special friends to the Choates.

Construction work was an important part of Ralph's missionary service. He was a fine carpenter and builder. His father had trained him well. In those years, none of the Africans knew how to do that type of work. "There's no other way to get the houses, workshops, schools, and churches we need except to do it ourselves," Ralph said.

Almost all of the buildings were made from clay bricks. Roofs were formed of long, tough grass tied into bundles. Ralph taught the workmen how to make the bricks and how to put them together into safe buildings.

He still used a cane, swinging his right leg and foot out in order to walk. However, he did not let this hinder him from doing what needed to be done. He helped lay the bricks. He climbed on top of buildings to tie the grass for the thatched roof. He built fine furniture, often from leftover wood and metal.

All who knew him said, "Ralph can fix anything from motorcycles to pots and pans."

He slept over one hundred nights at Mutaho by himself. When it was time for his family to move there, he was delighted. The one-room building made of poles and grass thatch was crowded. But at least the family was all together in one place.

"This house has problems," sighed Esther, soon after they moved. "First it was the leaky roof and the small creeks running through during the heavy rain. Now it's worms falling into our food."

In spite of the frustrations, Esther made the primitive little building into a cozy home. She created a bookcase out of boxes. Her clever hands fixed another box with a lid that could drop down to become a little writing desk. With a piece of eucalyptus limb and a glass tube that had once held a toothbrush, she formed an attractive vase.

Esther had equal ability to make their home beautiful outside. Mutaho station was located in the midst of twenty-seven acres that sloped gently toward the valley. A grove of eucalyptus trees stood between the buildings and the road. Esther and the workmen planted a lawn and many colorful flowers. She arranged a lily pool with graceful papyrus and calla lilies along the borders. Within sight of the house was a large patch of pineapple plants and several ranges of mountains. "A view worth a million dollars," Esther commented.

At first, the Africans at Mutaho were afraid of the Choates.

"We'll have to think of ways to help them get over their fear of white Protestants," Esther suggested.

God gave them an idea. On Sunday mornings they gathered up their little phonograph and several records of lively music. They took Bibles and songbooks and sat in the shade of the eucalyptus trees by the road. They turned the music on and waited for the Africans to pass by on their way to the Mutaho marketplace.

Choates tried to be casual and informal as people stopped to listen. When a few were standing around, not seeming to be afraid of them, Ralph and Esther stopped the phonograph and spoke a few words about Jesus. But the bystanders scattered quickly as soon as the white people spoke. The Choates continued anyway, singing and praying. Then they started the phonograph again, repeating the whole process.

Little by little the Africans were less fearful. The music was beginning to bring a crowd. After many Sundays, some stayed to listen for an entire morning.

Ralph and Esther decided it was time to hold a service inside a building. As the people arrived the first time, the missionaries were pleased. "Look!" they whispered to themselves. "So many came that they can't all crowd inside at once!"

Men and women as well as children enrolled in the first schools at Mutaho. The Africans enjoyed school and did not mind walking great distances, even in bad weather. Some of the children were from the Muslim religion. They did not know about Jesus. They studied the Bible courses right along with the others. They took active parts in the Christmas and Easter programs. They enjoyed vacation Bible school, too. Some of them said, "We'd like to be Christians." This made Ralph and Esther very happy.

It was not hard for the Choates to keep busy at the brand new station. An American publisher wrote to Ralph and asked, "Will you write a book about your experiences in Burundi?"

Ralph speedily replied, "No! We're too busy trying to keep up with just *having* the experiences."

Chapter 4

MEDICINE UNDER THE TREES

"It's here I feel the fire!" moaned an African with his arms wrapped around his waist.

"My eye won't open today," said another, showing Esther her swollen eyelid.

"I hear strange noises when I breathe," wheezed an elderly man.

Esther listened carefully to each complaint. Then she handed out the appropriate medicines. Sometimes she treated as many as 400 patients a day at her "shade tree dispensary."

People came to the eucalyptus grove with all sorts of ailments. Stomachaches, eye problems, bad coughs, and malaria were common. Dreadful sores called ulcers sometimes caused a leg to swell much more than its normal size. Because Africans did not wear shoes, she treated many injured toes, also. There were bad burns since the little round grass-covered huts easily caught on fire.

"I've had no nurse's training," Esther said. "My father taught me. He had learned all he could from doctors, but he had a God-given ability to treat illness and injury."

Several days a week she set up her medicines on the pole-and-reed table. Epsom salts and quinine, certain powders, and eye medicine were all kept in good supply in the big medicine box that was complete with shelves inside and a hinged lid that locked. Esther had her own particular recipe for cough medicine: honey with a dab of kerosene. Baking soda was added to make it fizz. (The soda also caused the kerosene to mix with the honey.) One teaspoonful was a dose. The patients liked it. "It helps our coughs!" they would always say.

The Africans knew and trusted Esther. Her love made them want to come back again and again.

Missionary life in Burundi was a pioneer adventure. There were no stores nearby for easy shopping. Convenience foods were not available. No handy appliances made the housewife's work easier. Esther and her houseboys did everything themselves.

"I need the help of houseboys or I wouldn't be able to find time for missionary work," Esther wrote to a friend.

These young Barundi houseboys were local schoolboys the Choates selected to help them. Often they had not learned to read yet. Many were not Christians when they started. Training them to help with housework and cooking was sometimes an ordeal for Esther.

"They've never heard about such a thing as a germ," she muttered one day. "And they haven't

used hot water and soap on dishes before. In fact, they don't know about cleanliness of any kind. There's so much for them to learn!"

Esther started them out with easy chores. They peeled potatoes and brought in firewood. Then they went on to learn about cooking on a stove and how to iron clothes.

Sometimes the boys got Esther's careful instructions mixed up. One of them served baked beans with fruit salad spread over the top for an evening meal. Esther took one look and said, "I'm sorry, children, but this is it for tonight!" Everyone at the table proved to be good sports and ate the unusual combination.

Once she found a houseboy stealing sugar. She talked to him about it. "Oh, no!" he replied solemnly. "I wasn't stealing. I was just giving it to myself."

Through the years, Esther trained many houseboys. After a long time, some of them developed into wonderful cooks and ironers.

No matter what happened, Ralph continued to be cheerful. He always had a joke to tell. He kept up with what was going on around the world by reading anything that was available. Photography and model trains were other interests.

Little things could make Ralph feel blessed . . . a pretty sunrise, the haunting duet of a papa and mama bell bird, a dove resting on a branch, listening and then cooing a reply as Ralph played his harmonica.

Music was important in the Choate household. Besides the harmonica, Ralph played the saxophone and flute. Esther learned to make pleasant music on the marimba. It was useful at prayer meetings and other church services.

Ralph and Esther were continually doing things to make other people happy.

"If you're near the Choates' home at bedtime or at mealtime, you'll be welcome there," everyone said.

People of many nations, missionaries, government officials, and the King and Queen of Burundi were all entertained graciously. It did not matter when they came, day or night. Everyone was welcomed whether they were invited or arrived unexpectedly. Sometimes the guests came for a short chat and cup of tea. Many stayed for a meal or two. Others remained for a few days or weeks.

Visitors soon discovered Esther could create a wonderful meal at a moment's notice. Her melt-in-your-mouth biscuits and tasty pineapple pie were famous.

Younger missionaries called Ralph and Esther "Pa" and "Ma." Unmarried missionaries were included as part of the family. They all appreciated the friendship and counsel the Choates offered.

"I'm about ready to pack my things and go back home," Betty Schultz, a missionary from World Gospel Mission, once told Esther. "It's just too hard here."

"Why did you come in the first place?" Esther inquired.

"The Lord wanted me to."

"Did He tell you to go home?"

"Well, no," Betty answered.

Esther patted her friend on the shoulder and said gently, "Then you'd better stay until He does."

Esther's encouragement was exactly what was needed. Betty Schultz served God in Burundi for many years.

Larry and Ann were continually an important part of Ralph and Esther's life. "God has given them to us and we will take care of them in the best way we know how," they determined. The children traveled right along wherever their parents went. They easily became part of the missionary work.

Esther sewed clothes for the children. She and Ralph had fun planning and making gifts for them. Every day they read the Bible and prayed with Larry and Ann. "Whatever God wants you to do, do it well," Ralph and Esther admonished.

Evenings were special family times for reading together, going for walks, or just sitting on the porch listening to the sounds of evening.

"Play marimba music for us to go to sleep by," Larry and Ann sometimes begged. Then they would settle comfortably into their beds as Esther softly played their favorite songs.

The Mutaho mission station grew as God blessed the work. Hundreds of students were enrolled in the schools. The chapel could no longer hold all who came to the Sunday morning worship services. More than 36,000 patients had already been treated at Esther's "shade tree dispensary."

The Barundi women were learning how to obey God. "We want to get rid of our heathen charms," they said. "These little sticks and bundles of powder wrapped in banana leaves don't protect us from sickness. They don't help us have babies, either. God wants us to trust Him."

"You'll fall over dead if you burn the charms," warned their friends and family.

Even so, some of the Christian women chose to burn their homemade charms, after a Sunday morning service. No one fell over dead. Instead, God blessed the brave Christians.

The Friends Africa Gospel Mission gave a section of land to World Gospel Mission. "It will be good for you to have a school there at Murore (Moo-ROAR-aye)," Ralph said.

Other missionaries came to help. There was more than enough work for all of them. Every day was a busy day!

Ralph and Esther loved the Barundi more and more. They felt blessed and happy with all God was doing.

They had no idea of the difficult days that were coming!

Chapter 5

HUNGRY PEOPLE

"God wants you to put away all sin. You need to get rid of everything that has to do with the devil." Seekers at the Sunday afternoon service listened eagerly as Ralph preached.

After the message, one of the African men gave his testimony. "God came near and washed away my sins. He took the trash out of my heart. He filled my heart with His forgiveness. Now I am a new man."

Prayer time was next. "O God, my Father, I come before Thee just now," a man prayed. "Hear me and give pardon for my sins. Take my arms and lead me as a shepherd leads his cows and calves. Don't let me go, but run off the devil and shake him into the valley or river."

It had been five years since Ralph and Esther started the work at Mutaho. Now, many people were asking God to forgive them. They wanted to obey Him. Several had become members of the

Mutaho church. Others were studying so they could become members later.

Then came a very hard time in the life of the Friends Africa Gospel Mission.

The Barundi had planted seeds in their little farm plots just as they did every season. However, this time the rains did not come. The seeds could not grow.

The people planted seeds again. Still the rains did not come. All of the spare food was used up by that time.

People were hungry! In fact, they were starving to death!

Early in 1944 the schools closed. Thirty people had already died from starvation near Kibimba. Ralph wrote about it in his diary.

March 22: A government official brought a ton of bean seed to sell to the needy people. It was sold to 216 people.

March 31: At Kibimba we missionaries are cooking food and serving it to about 200 people a day. The folks here are really suffering because they don't have enough food.

April 19: We are now feeding 500 people every day. More have died.

Ralph and Esther spent many days at Kibimba helping the other missionaries provide food for the starving Barundi, who were too weak to help themselves. After a while they were cooking for over a thousand people. Seeing so many Barundi that near

to death each day was almost more than the missionaries could stand.

For ten days, Ralph drove the mission truck to Bujumbura every day. Each time he brought back sixty-five bags of cassava flour or shelled peanuts. Immediately the hungry people lined up to receive their small portions.

Then came the long-awaited day when it began to rain. Soon the nightmare of the famine was past. But by then, over 10,000 Africans had starved to death.

*　　*　　*

"There's going to be a big missionary conference here at Mutaho," Ralph announced soon after the famine. "There'll be missionaries from the Church of England, World Gospel Mission, Danish Baptists, and Free Methodists. Including us Friends, there'll be about one hundred altogether."

Esther enlisted the help of the missionary ladies from Kibimba to make cookies. Dozens and dozens of the treats were baked and safely sealed in tin containers, ready for afternoon tea.

Ralph was busy with preparations outside. He built little box-shaped huts out among the trees behind the house. Guests would sleep there. He trimmed the grass all around and hired Africans to carry water, give out firewood, and help in other ways.

The guests arranged to cook for themselves. As they arrived, they received fresh meat, eggs, and vegetables. Fifty-one cows provided milk every day, both morning and evening.

One day during the conference, Ralph and Esther issued a special invitation. "Please come to a good old American hamburger feed." Ralph formed a huge pyramid of hamburger patties while Esther baked batch after batch of feathery-light biscuits.

"These are wonderful!" exclaimed the missionary guests, many of whom had never eaten an American hamburger before. "Let's do it again!"

The Choates agreed, and served hamburgers once more before the conference was ended.

*   *   *

When Larry and Ann reached school age, Esther taught them at home. Besides their studies, they often had strange and fascinating pets to occupy their time. Wimpy, a chimpanzee who belonged to another missionary, visited for one year. Two monkeys named Jughead and Chipper were favorites. At times, antelopes were part of the family, but it was a small wildcat that became Larry's special pet.

Occasionally the government school inspector came to visit. He often was invited to stay for lunch. During one of these noontime meals, there was an unexpected interruption.

Drip! Drip! Drip!

Soon, a little puddle glistened in the middle of the table.

Esther looked up and then down! Ralph looked down and then up! "Oh, no!" they said, feeling very embarrassed.

The government inspector first looked up, then around at the others.

"It's Larry's pet wildcat," they explained. Their faces turned the color of ripe tomatoes. "He's up above the ceiling mat. He . . . er . . . a . . . apparently he . . . he doesn't have very good manners!"

Their guest began to laugh. Ralph and Esther scurried around to clean up the mess. After a while they, too, had a good laugh.

*   *   *

"You are needed at home. Mrs. Chilson is very ill."

This urgent message reached Ralph and Esther while they were on a work vacation in 1945.

"Yes, we'll go immediately," they agreed. They lost no time in getting their things loaded into the pickup truck and heading back to Kibimba. Two other missionaries went along, also.

"Oh, no! Look at that python!" exclaimed Ralph. The huge snake with gold, tan, and brown patterned skin was like a log blocking the road. "We'll have to take time to kill it. We don't want it going into the villages and killing any of the children."

"Or eating the goats that belong to the villagers, either," reminded one of the others.

Ralph shifted gears and forced the pickup to bump back and forth across the snake. The others threw rocks at its head. In a little while they could see that the snake was dead.

"Fourteen feet long!" Ralph pronounced as he rolled out the tape measure. "At least it won't harm anyone now!"

Mrs. Chilson remained ill for five months. Early on Christmas day the family gathered close beside her bed. In a few minutes they knew she had gone to Heaven.

Ralph supervised the funeral service and burial. It was a sad day for all who knew her. "Her dedication to God's work in Africa will always be remembered," people said.

Ralph and Esther had been in Burundi for ten years. Life there had been busy but satisfying. "We're glad we are doing what God wants us to do," they said.

Now it was time for them to go back to the United States for their first furlough.

"Remember, we love you and we will be praying for you," they told the Africans. "And we will be back soon."

Choates'
first home
at Kibimba

African woman
grinding grain

43

Bell tower at
Kibimba;
workshop-garage-
storeroom under
construction

Larry and
Ann Choate,
holding a
snake skin

Chapter 6

THE KIBIMBA REBELLION

For the first time, Larry and Ann saw the United States they had heard so much about. They met Grandpa and Grandma Choate, aunts, uncles, and cousins. The good English their parents had carefully taught them came in handy. They discovered why it had been important for them to learn proper manners.

During this year at home, Ralph and Esther had opportunity to visit many churches. They talked about the ways God had blessed the Friends Africa Gospel Mission. They also told people, "Sometimes life is hard there. But God is always with us."

Ralph, along with missionaries from other Protestant missions, began to make plans for a special school where Africans could be taught how to be teachers. "This will be a teacher-training college. We'll use the French words for teacher-training college and name the new school *Ecole de Moniteurs*," the planners announced.

The group decided that Kibimba would be a suitable location for the college. Then they chose Ralph Choate to be responsible for seeing that the school was established.

"I will need to go to school again myself," he decided. "There are things I should learn before we begin the new college. Things the government says I need to know."

When their year of furlough was over, the Choates told about their plans. "Ralph will go to Belgium for a year of special study while Esther and the children return to Burundi."

For the next year, Ralph studied hard in Belgium. He learned the French language. Part of the time he spent in visiting schools there. During those twelve months he learned many helpful things.

After he returned to Burundi, he worked to get everything ready for the school. Ralph planned the classes he and others would teach. Missionary men worked hard to construct the buildings.

When the preparations were finished, forty-six young men arrived from many Protestant mission stations. For the next five years they studied and worked together. All but four or five of them completed the course. (One of those was asked to leave because he went back to witchcraft. One or two did not do very good work, and one died.)

Many years later Ralph attended an important meeting with African men from other Protestant missions. He was pleased to see that seven of the men present were graduates of that first class of the *Ecole*

de Moniteurs. After that, some became government officials. He was glad to know that all of their hard work had been worthwhile.

The college eventually grew to an enrollment of 400 students. There were new buildings, better equipment, and a good teaching staff. Most of the teachers were the Africans themselves. "This is what we had always dreamed about and prayed for," the missionaries said.

*   *   *

The years at the teachers' college went by fast. Once again it was time for the Choates to go back to the United States.

"This trip will be a special one," Ralph said to his family. "It will be the last time we will be taking a trip like this together."

They flew from Burundi to Italy. They rode a train through Europe, enjoying wonderful experiences none of them would ever have again. They traveled on the huge ocean liner *Queen Mary* from England to New York. The entire journey was long remembered by all of them.

Ralph visited his parents in Oregon. It was the last time he saw his mother. In September, Ralph and Esther helped Ann settle into school at Haviland, Kansas. Larry was enrolled in school at Wichita for a few months. Then he, too, would go to Haviland.

Sadly they parted from each other. All four of them knew that life would never be the same in the future.

*   *   *

As soon as they arrived back at Mutaho, Ralph and Esther were once again in charge. There was more than enough to keep them busy.

Ralph directed the large group of workmen who assisted with building projects. He also taught school, pulled teeth, wrote letters, and kept the money affairs straight for the mission station.

"I wonder what will happen tomorrow?" he sometimes said at night. "There certainly hasn't been a dull moment today."

Ralph felt concerned because the older men were not coming to church on Sunday. "We can't," they told him. "We have to stay home and herd our cattle."

"You know the pasture I have fenced in?" Ralph asked. "You just herd your cows up here to church. Open the gate and put 'em inside. Then shut the gate and come along to church and listen to the sermon."

After that, there were as many as three or four small herds of cattle in the pasture every Sunday morning. Ralph was happy the men could hear the messages after all.

Esther taught classes, entertained guests, translated literature into Kirundi, and did medical work. She supervised the gardening, and was still an excellent homemaker. Life was not dull for her, either.

"It's twenty-five years since the Chilsons first came to Burundi," Ralph reminded the others in the spring of 1958.

"We'll have an anniversary celebration," the missionaries decided. "One day of celebration and four days of revival meetings."

Dates were chosen and invitations were sent to the King of Burundi, to all the chiefs, other important leaders, and business people. The missionaries planned food for the officials and missionary guests. Members of the church collected money to buy food for the lunch they would serve to the African visitors.

Just when everything was all set, serious problems developed at Kibimba. The anniversary celebration had to be canceled!

"We want to drink the sweet beer made from banana juice," declared some of the African Christians. "We want to have more than one wife. We also don't want to pay our tithe anymore."

The Kibimba rebellion was underway!

49

The missionaries were sad. Even so, they listened to the demands. They met with groups of Christians from the mission stations.

"Those actions would not please God," they reminded the people. "It is better to obey Him." They did their best to explain again what the Bible said about such matters.

However, the church members were determined to have their own way. Some of the African teachers in the mission schools refused to go to work. Government officials came to help settle the problems. There was almost a riot during one meeting at Kibimba.

Through these troublesome weeks, many of the African pastors encouraged the missionaries. "We love you," they said. "We do not approve of what these church members are doing. We will stay true to God."

Unfortunately, 700 of their members said, "We don't want to be church members anymore. We'll do things our own way."

Ralph and Esther and the other Friends missionaries continued to love the Barundi. "Dear God, please help them turn back to You," they prayed.

After a while the situation improved. Special meetings at many of the stations brought spiritual revival. The Kibimba rebellion appeared to be over.

"Now we can have the anniversary celebration," the mission staff concluded. Another date was chosen and the invitations went out. Plans were underway for the second time.

In spite of all that had happened, the occasion turned out to be worthwhile.

"We are happy that your mission has helped the people of Burundi in so many ways," a government leader said in his speech. "We offer our best wishes for the next twenty-five years."

Others spoke about the medical work, the schools, and the churches. They recalled the names of the thirty-five Friends missionaries who had helped through the years. They sadly remembered one of them, Eli Wheeler, who had died in a hunting accident there.

After special music and a message, Pastor Simon Sodiya closed the occasion with prayer.

"So much has happened in these last twenty-five years," said Ralph that night.

Esther smiled. "And who knows what may be ahead in the next twenty-five? Or even what tomorrow will bring? One thing is sure, though, God will never leave us nor forsake us, no matter what is happening all around us!"

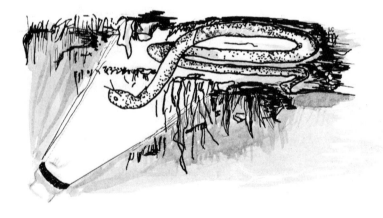

Chapter 7

A SNAKE
ON THE PATH

"I'm going out to the workshop to turn off the light generator," Ralph informed Esther. He headed for the door, then stopped. "Oh, oh! This flashlight's not working very well."

Retracing his steps into the kitchen, he took time to fix the light. "There, that's better!" he thought.

Once outside, he pointed the flashlight straight down the gravel path. Immediately he saw the danger!

Directly in the middle of the pool of light was a deadly black mamba snake. It was standing high, twisted into a big S, ready to strike. Ralph's foot was only inches away.

Instantly he stepped high and wide. Then, almost in the same motion, he swiftly whirled and whacked the snake vigorously with his cane.

Whack! Whack! Thump, thump!

Others heard the commotion and dashed out to investigate. A few more whacks and Ralph stopped.

The snake lay still. Cautiously the men examined the black mamba, one of the world's most poisonous snakes. "It's dead now!" Their voices were shaky with fear.

"Are *you* all right?" someone asked, looking anxiously at Ralph.

"Yes!" he murmured, somewhat breathlessly.

"That's the fourth snake like that we've killed around here lately," Esther observed. Her voice was shaky, too. "Thank the Lord you took time to fix the flashlight!"

* * *

That same year, Esther received a special invitation from the World Gospel Mission missionaries. "Please come to be one of the speakers for the Women's Conference at Murehe (Moo-RAY-hay)."

Ralph and Esther prayed about it. Then she replied, "Yes, I will come."

Margaret Thompson, a rather new WGM missionary, was the other speaker. "I'm not an expert in Kirundi like you are," she said to Esther. "I don't feel very confident yet about preaching in that language."

In her usual encouraging manner, Esther answered, "Remember, knowing the language isn't everything. You must have the power of God's spirit. Otherwise you won't be effective, no matter how well you know the language. Go ahead, Margaret. Preach the message that God has given you."

God answered prayer and blessed both mission-ary women as they preached. The conference for the African women turned out to be helpful to all who attended.

Esther told Ralph about it when she got back to Mutaho. Knowing how much he loved animals, she added, "You'd be interested in the pets the mission-aries had." She described Skippy the monkey, as well as Christopher and Ichabod the long-legged cranes. She told about Never More and Yard Bird, the ravens who talked and stole everything not fastened down.

"There was an eagle named Evil Eye." She laughed as she remembered his tricks. "He's too lazy to kill his own food. He sat on a pole and screamed until someone brought food to him."

*   *   *

Just before Christmas, Ralph announced his plans to go to Bujumbura on a shopping trip. The capital city was almost the only place where they could buy necessities. Reta Stuart, a Friends missionary who was living with the Choates, said she would go along.

"We'll take a different route," said Ralph, as he headed the car cross-country instead of along the usual road.

The different route turned out to be the wrong route. They tried another road. It was wrong, too. After that they came to a bridge that was washed out.

"I think I made the wrong decision," said Ralph. He turned the car around. The steep, narrow, rough trails that were not really roads at all, twisted and turned this way and that.

What a relief when at last they came to the main road!

As soon as they got to the city, Ralph hurried to cash a check. Reta gave him money for gas. He jammed the packet of money in his left shirt pocket and stayed in the car to wait while Reta shopped.

"Look here! We have a beautiful beaded belt!" exclaimed an African man, leaning through the open right front window. "Buy it!"

Ralph looked at the belt. "It's nice, but too short for me." Three other African men stepped around by the open left window. "I don't think I'll buy it!" Ralph repeated to the man on the right.

Just then he felt the packet of money slide out of his pocket. Ralph's hands flew up to grab the thief. It was too late! The thief was already running down the street behind the car.

As soon as Reta returned, Ralph drove up and down the street. The men were nowhere to be seen. "Well!" said Ralph disgustedly. "Somewhere around here there's a man who's twenty-four dollars richer than he was a few minutes ago."

*　　*　　*

Ralph and Esther spent several months during 1961 and 1962 on furlough in the United States. They attended Ann's graduation from nursing school. Two days later they were pleased to be present for her wedding to Gary Fuqua.

Before going back to Burundi, Ralph said good-bye to his father. "I'll not see you again," Calvin Choate said. (Before Ralph and Esther came home the next time they received word that Mr. Choate had died.)

They arrived back in Burundi just in time to help celebrate a very important occasion—Independence Day. At last this small country was no longer under the rule of Belgium. It now belonged to the Barundi themselves.

At Kibimba there was a simple Independence Day service on July 2. The Belgian flag was removed. The red, green, and white Burundi flag with three red stars in the middle was raised in its place.

As soon as Independence Day was over, Ralph and Esther began to settle in their new location at Mweya (MWAY-uh).

This mission station was twenty-four miles southeast of Kibimba. It was located in territory served by the Free Methodist mission. Several years before, a Bible school opened there on the hill. Many Africans came to the classes. Nearby was the school for missionary children. The Free Methodists, World Gospel Mission, and Friends worked together to organize and maintain these schools.

"I'm going to call this place Windy Hill," Esther announced. "The wind always blows up here."

Ralph and Esther began their new adventures as dorm parents. From fifteen to twenty missionary children lived there during the school year. Besides making a home-away-from-home for the children, the Choates also taught at the Bible School.

Ralph taught twenty-seven classes each week. Esther taught just part of the time. Many other tasks filled her days. She made bread, tended the vegetable and flower gardens, did laundry, darned socks, and patched clothes. Also she made sure the children completed their assigned tasks. The houseboys were under her direction, too.

Esther provided a small plot of ground for each child to have his or her own garden. One student grew a squash so big the cook made fourteen pies from it.

Friday night at Windy Hill was "fun night." The children were allowed to stay up later than usual. Sunday afternoons Esther organized hikes and visits to African homes. Sometimes she led a swimming party to the river.

Uncle Ralph and Aunt Esther, as they were called, maintained a good balance of strictness and fun. The children always knew the Choates loved them.

"We're like one big family," they often said. For the missionary children, it was next best to being at home with their parents.

As happy as they were, Ralph and Esther began to realize during the last of the six years they lived at Mweya, that heartaches might soon be added to their blessings.

Chapter 8

HEARTACHES

On May 1, 1965, Ralph Choate wrote these words: "Within ten days the local elections begin. There is a strong feeling between two groups of the people. Whichever wins the election, it is possible that our peace might be rudely shattered. We can only pray."

Things happened as the missionaries feared. The elections brought the beginning of real heartaches for everyone.

For over 300 years the Batutsi had been the rulers. They planned to continue. However, the elections raised many of the Bahutu into places of leadership.

The Batutsi no longer had complete control. They did not like what was happening. Right away they did their best to get rid of non-Batutsi leaders, as well as anyone who *might* be a leader in the future. Someone shot and wounded the Prime Minister of Burundi. Other leaders disappeared and were not heard from again. Thousands of Africans were killed.

Schoolwork at the mission stations went very slowly. Some were searched. Tension was high among students and teachers. Word got around that a few of the Bahutu leaders had been imprisoned.

Officials at the American embassy in Bujumbura did not know how far the trouble might extend. They were worried about the missionaries. "You must be ready to leave the country very quickly," they warned.

Ralph and Esther continued their work as best they could. They prayed and trusted God.

News came about missionaries who had been forced to leave Burundi with only a few hours notice. "Will we be next?" the others wondered.

And then, to add to the problems, Ralph felt pains in his chest. I'm afraid it may be the beginning of heart trouble," he said.

In the midst of the difficult days, welcome news came from their daughter Ann and her husband, Gary Fuqua. "We have been appointed as missionaries to Burundi," they wrote. "We will be there sometime next summer." Ralph and Esther could hardly wait until that time.

The trouble continued for a long time. Many of the Bahutu leaders were already dead. Others had fled to safety in a neighboring country. It was easy for the Batutsi to once again be in control, now that their top enemies were out of the way.

The worrisome political situation quieted and life became more normal for the missionaries. "Perhaps the trouble is over for good," they said with hope.

The wonderful day came when the Fuquas arrived. Ralph and Esther were grateful to have them nearby.

*   *   *

"At last! It's done!" The entire Kirundi Bible!" exclaimed Esther.

For a long time, a missionary named Rosemary Buillebaud from England had been translating the Bible into Kirundi. Esther and other missionaries had helped with the proofreading. They had also tested it with the Africans to see if they could understand the translation.

"We'll give a Kirundi Bible to each of our Bible school students," Ralph announced. Since he was the director of the Mweya Bible School that year, he and the young men organized programs to help people understand the importance of the new Kirundi Bible. "Now you must take the Bible out to every Protestant mission station," Ralph encouraged. "We want everyone to buy it and read it."

Soon after that, Ralph and Esther went on furlough again. While they were home, Ralph was honored to receive a Doctor of Letters degree from George Fox College.

"We recognize the important work you are doing for God there in Burundi," College officials told him.

Next, the Choates spent three wonderful months with Larry, his wife Dee, and their children, Cathy, Larry Junior, Lonny, and Candy. Ralph and Esther relished the privilege of riding with Dee as she drove a school bus and with Larry as the driver of a great Greyhound bus.

"How good it is to see our loved ones serving the Lord in their daily work," they said to one another.

Time flew by and soon they were back in Burundi. They settled into a house in Gitega, a small town in the very center of the country.

Earlier, representatives from the Friends, Free Methodists, and World Gospel Mission had cooperatively signed official papers, purchasing the Burundi Literature Center. Now Ralph and Esther were selected to manage the Christian bookshop, which also sold gifts and curios.

Many people came into the store every week. They were anxious to buy the religious literature that was printed in four languages, or the Bibles that were available in nine languages.

One month, Ralph was especially interested in the sales record. "Esther, do you realize we sold a lot of French New Testaments and Kirundi Bibles to the Catholics for their schools? They bought more than anyone else."

"That's because they've been given permission to use the Protestant Bible," she replied. "The Catholic Bible isn't translated into Kirundi yet."

Ralph and Esther were pleased with the work in Gitega. They were also happily anticipating Gary and Ann's first baby, due to be born in two months.

Then came the night of December 16!

The baby arrived prematurely. Fear gripped the anxious grandparents. However, they felt better when the doctor said, "Everything seems to be okay."

Next morning Ralph drove back to Gitega. At noon he listened carefully to the Friends radio broadcast. He heard Paul Thornburg report, "I'm so sorry to announce that the beautiful baby girl born last night to Ann and Gary died a few moments ago."

Ralph sat there quietly. He did not want to believe what he had just heard.

Missionary friends from all around came to comfort the Choates and the Fuquas.

With love in their hearts, Ralph and Esther helped place Marlys Ann Fuqua's tiny coffin in a grave near those of her great-grandparents, Arthur and Edna Chilson.

(North of the Kibimba church, the little cemetery is enclosed by a brick wall. The gates are kept shut so wandering cattle and grazing goats will not interfere. The graves are sheltered by evergreen trees. A fresh breeze blows through openings in the wall. A few wild flowers are bright dots here and there. There are five bronze markers to reflect the noonday sun. One bears the name of Wheeler, two the name of Chilson. The other two say Fuqua, for

in a few years Marlys Ann was joined in Heaven by a little brother named Shawn Nduwayo, the Kirundi name meaning "I am His.")

Even though they felt very sad, Ralph and Esther went back to their work. They were strengthened as concerned Barundi friends showed their deep love and respect. One day a pastor who had been a student at Mweya Bible School came to visit. "Perhaps God up there in Heaven found a grandmother who had recently come to Heaven and was lonely," he suggested. "Perhaps God asked Marlys Ann to come back to Heaven so this grandmother would have a baby to care for."

The Choates felt comforted!

With that comfort and continued faith in God, they were soon to face situations that horrified people all around the world!

Chapter 9

TROUBLE
STRIKES AGAIN

Nothing had ever prevented Ralph from plunging ahead with his work. On August 25, 1970, however, he stopped abruptly! Right away he was admitted to the hospital in Bujumbura.

"You have suffered a heart attack," the doctor announced.

Esther thought about the hard work Ralph had recently finished. He had exerted strenuous effort as he hammered and sawed a damaged church door back into usefulness. She felt sure the work combined with the last difficult years had helped to bring on the attack.

Fortunately, Ralph's heart responded to the treatments. After eleven days, the doctor said, "He may go home now."

Gradually he recovered his strength. During this time he began using the wheelchair graciously sent by friends in the United States. It was good that he did not have to walk from where they lived in one end of the long building to the Literature Center located at the opposite end.

*   *   *

Through the years in Burundi, Ralph and Esther were invited to many special celebrations. They attended programs, teas, luncheons, dinners, weddings, and receptions honoring important people. Ralph liked to take photographs of such events. They enjoyed visiting with the fascinating people.

They listened with interest as exciting news spread quickly throughout the town of Gitega. "Emperor Haile (HIGH-lee) Selassie (Sah-LAS-sie) of Ethiopia will come soon. All of the shops are to close for the day. Everyone is ordered to attend the celebration that will be held at the stadium."

The townspeople got busy right away. Painters freshened up the buildings. Workmen hung copies of the Emperor's pictures all about town. Flags fluttered from poles and posts. People made evergreen wreaths and flower garlands to decorate windows and doorways. The town was in a festive mood.

On the morning of the occasion, Ralph and Esther arrived at the stadium early. "I want to get some good pictures," Ralph said.

A huge crowd soon gathered. At the proper time, two helicopters whirred their way onto the field.

The crowd suddenly grew silent. The famous Emperor Haile Selassie stepped out of the helicopter. He waved to the crowd, who waved back.

The program was filled with speeches and music. There was a fine show of drumming, dancing, and tumbling.

Ralph leaned over and whispered to Esther. "Know what this reminds me of? The time when the real King, Jesus Christ, will come back to earth again."

Esther nodded. "If only the people would be this excited about His coming. But that's why we're here, isn't it? To help them know about Him and look forward to the time He'll come again."

*   *   *

The problems that began in 1965 had not completely disappeared as everyone had hoped. Now, seven years later, the Bahutu banded together again, trying once more to gain authority. The Batutsi struck back, wanting to rid the country of all Africans who might take away their power. The same horrible things happened as before, only this time it was worse.

All of the missionary work was close to a standstill. Ralph kept careful record of the appalling details.

April 22: Roadblock barriers are up around Gitega. We have to have road passes in order to go anywhere.

April 30: I was not allowed to drive the car all the way to church today. We were stopped at a barrier at the edge of Gitega. The car was searched. The others walked on to church while I brought the car home.

May 1: We have to get permission in order to buy kerosene and gasoline now. We listen carefully to all radio news.

May 14: We hear reports that 8,000 people are dead. We believe that all of the Friends who were caught were killed.

May 16: We heard long bursts of gunfire from the prison close by. Our hearts are like lead weights inside of us.

May 17: Gary and Ann report from Kwisumo (Kwee-SUE-moe) that they are okay. Things seem to be calm in their area.

May 19: There's been trouble at Mweya. One student was beaten and another questioned.

May 20: Kibimba medical assistants are all either dead or in hiding.

May 22: Since we live close to the government offices, Esther spends a lot of her time up there requesting road permits and fuel purchase permits for missionaries. We refused to hide radios and other valuables for Africans. There was a lot of booming and shooting just before dark.

May 23: There was a fight at the army camp at breakfast time. I think it's best to keep the Literature Center closed again.

May 24: The Literature Center was open for business, the first time for a week.

May 25: Gary and Ann arrived safely in Gitega. They had to pass through eleven barrier inspection points.

May 28: There was much gunfire at the prison.

June 7: Two or three truckloads of students from the Kilemba station school in southern Burundi were killed. They were from the Swedish Pentecostal Mission.

July 24: The killings continue.

Finally there was a more cheerful note on August 15: Today is our wedding anniversary. I gave Esther a wristwatch. She had bought a billfold made out of elephant leather for me.

"Why don't you smile and look happy?" a soldier asked Esther.

"Looking happy in these days isn't easy," she replied solemnly.

After many more months of violence and tragedy, things began to slowly improve. Early in 1973, Ralph wrote, "This is the first time in over a year there are no police barriers and road checks."

Missionaries from every denomination were heartbroken. Many pastors had died. Churches were without leaders. Schools had no teachers. The little country of Burundi would never completely recover from the terrible things that had occurred.

*   *   *

"We will be back," Ralph and Esther promised as they left Burundi to return to the United States in 1974. It was time for a rest. Also, they wanted to be home in time for the birth of Ann and Gary Fuqua's third child.

On May 14, Leslie Lynn Iranzi (Kirundi, meaning "God knows me") was born in Wichita, Kansas.

69

She was healthy and much loved by her Grandpa and Grandma Choate.

Twelve days later, Esther received a distinctive honor. "Because of your faithful commitment and service to God, we are pleased to award you this Doctor of Public Service degree," said the president of Friends University during the ceremony.

Ralph and Esther visited many of the congregations that had been so faithful in praying for them during their forty years of missionary service. "Thank you for praying for us," they told their friends. "Your prayers were important, and God answered them. Keep praying for us. We will be going back to Burundi soon."

Then, surprisingly, they began to wonder, "Is it really right for us to return?"

They talked with Friends church leaders in Wichita. Together they prayed about it. "We have worked two years past the usual time for retiring," Ralph and Esther pointed out.

It was disappointing for them to think they might not go back to Africa. But finally the decision was made.

"We feel that we should not return to Burundi," they announced bravely. "It is time for us to retire from missionary service."

Immediately they began the process of learning how to live permanently in the United States.

Chapter 10

HAPPY MEMORIES

Esther looked out of the window of their almost-new mobile home in Maize, Kansas. She turned and smiled at Ralph. "Guess who just drove in? Ann and little Leslie. Isn't it wonderful to live so near!"

Ralph agreed. Larry and his wife, Dee, along with three of their children, lived in the Northwest. Even that was closer than they had been for a long time. Ralph and Esther's other grandson and his wife were just two hours down the road at Haviland. It was good to get acquainted with family members they had seen so few times in the last twenty years.

"Look what I discovered," Esther said. She held out a coin for Ann to see.

"It's the original nickel she found on the road in Greenleaf, Idaho," Ralph explained. "The one that started our Africa fund. We've kept it all these years."

"Little did we know what was ahead of us when we put it in the little clay cup from Africa," said Esther.

"But what a wonderful life it's been!" Ralph added.

It was easy for the happy memories to come tumbling out, one after another.

Ralph picked up a box of pictures. "Just think of all the trips we've taken. Vacations, work trips, journeys to and from our furloughs—more miles than we ever dreamed possible!"

They reminisced about their vacation in Albert Park. "That was the time we saw fifty-six elephants and hundreds of hippos," Ralph remembered.

"And antelopes along with wild pigs, too. Plus about 200 buffalo," Esther added.

"We drove through the park one other time at night," Ralph reminded them. "That's definitely not recommended. Remember how we almost ran into the hippo that came charging down the hill?"

They discovered they had not forgotten another dark night when they saw the eyes of a giraffe glowing like hot coals. Laughing, Ralph said, "At first we thought there were two fires out on the hillside. Then we found out it wasn't a hill at all. Just a long-necked giraffe with bright shining eyes!"

Memories came back of trips by ship on the Atlantic, Pacific, and Indian oceans. And on seas called Tyrrhenian, Mediterranean, Red, and Caribbean. Big ships, little boats, good or stormy weather, fine meals, strange foods . . . Ralph and Esther had experienced them all.

There were lots of memories of slow trips on land and water. They thought about the fast flights by air. Times came to mind of breakfast in one country, supper in another, with travel through two or three others in between.

"But let me tell you, Ann," said Ralph seriously. "At the end of all those journeys there was hard work, some heartaches, much happiness, and many blessings. We never knew what tomorrow would bring, but *always* there was a deep satisfaction in being in the will of the Lord."

One memory seemed to lead right into another.

"Easter was always a highlight to me," Ralph recalled. "I remember how we'd get up early, at least a half hour before sunrise. Already we'd been hearing the voices and laughter of the Christians walking in from all directions for the service."

Esther smiled as Ralph continued. "We'd dress quickly. Then with flashlights and maybe a lantern we'd go along the path through the orchard to the east entrance of the church."

"I always loved the sounds of those early Easter mornings," said Esther, picking up the remembrance. "Birds chirping and the chattering of the African Christians. The breeze was usually chilly, and the stars would shine through clear spots between the clouds."

After that, the three laughed about the Christmas parties. "The houseboys always consumed an amazing number of Esther's good cookies," Ralph pointed out. "Dishpans full of 'em, all pink, yellow, and green frosted. At one party the boys ate eight or ten apiece, I'm sure. What a great time they had!"

There were thoughts of dispensary days, when medicines were kindly given out under the shade trees. "The general health of our Africans greatly improved," they reminded themselves. People lived longer and felt better. More babies survived, too. Lots of times the people would say, "Kibimba medicine makes us get well." Everyone knew that the Africans preferred being treated by the missionaries rather than by government doctors.

Esther laughingly told about the day Ralph mistakenly bought 144 jars of powdered coffee all at once. Then Ralph described the little aprons Esther made for the African children. "You see," he explained to Ann, "They didn't wear anything to school but their smiles. These colorful aprons made them well dressed for the programs, anyway."

"We enjoyed you and Larry so much," Esther remarked warmly. "You were never a burden to us. It was always a joy to have you be part of our work." The years of close family life had been a real blessing to both parents and children.

"You two were excellent examples to us," Ann commented. "Your lives have helped Larry and me know how to raise our own families."

They remembered their delightful friends among leaders of Burundi. "And how we loved our missionary friends, too," said Ann. "You know, Larry and I had more friends than most children who grow up here in the United States. Friends from all around the world! Now that's a real privilege."

More and more happy memories came to mind. It was plain to see there were enough stored up to last a lifetime.

However, life as retired missionaries had more to offer Ralph and Esther than just happy memories.

They had always helped wherever they were needed. To them, God's work was a way of life, not something one did just part of the time.

Esther took on a new job. Her love for children was evident as she aided handicapped children who rode on a school bus. God had given her a special way with those needing help.

She and Ralph volunteered to work together at the church office a few hours each month. They were pleased when they received letters from their loyal Barundi Friends.

Ralph got out their excellent diaries and started working on a book about their years in Burundi. "For our children and grandchildren," he said. He continued to enjoy photography.

Ralph and Esther Choate will always be remembered for their loving, caring, capable, self-sacrificing, and hospitable ways.

Esther's special gifts in language, medical work, and homemaking will not be forgotten. Ralph's unfailing cheerfulness has impressed all who know him. His good mind for details and unique skills in building are evident throughout Burundi. All who knew him at the primary schools, the Teacher Training College, and at Mweya Bible School appreciate his teaching abilities. From the time he began teaching in 1931, he discovered it was no disgrace to say, "I don't know the answer to your question. But I shall find the answer and have it for you in a day or two."

In September 1984, Reta Stuart, friend and co-worker, wrote these words in tribute to Ralph and Esther Choate: "They had touched many lives there, Africans and others. That ministry goes on here, though, and they have adjusted well to life in the United States. They were missionary pioneers, in many ways. They were 'parents' to a lot of us. But most of all, they have been friends—ours and God's."

With love in their hearts, Ralph and Esther declare, "God has fulfilled His promise never to leave us nor forsake us. To our dying days we shall praise Him for His faithfulness."

FROM THE WRITER . . .

A special "thank you" goes to members of the Choate family and other missionaries who were so generous with their time and information, helping to make this book become a reality.

Writing about Ralph and Esther has been a privilege; I have known them as long as I can remember. The Choate family were special friends of my mother when she was a young woman. Calvin Choate, Ralph's father, was her pastor. Many years later he performed the wedding ceremony for my husband, Gene, and me. I thank the Lord for the valuable contribution this family has made to my life.   —Betty M. Hockett